EXAMINING TSA'S CADRE OF CRIMINAL INVESTIGATORS

HEARING

BEFORE THE

SUBCOMMITTEE ON TRANSPORTATION SECURITY

OF THE

COMMITTEE ON HOMELAND SECURITY HOUSE OF REPRESENTATIVES

ONE HUNDRED THIRTEENTH CONGRESS

SECOND SESSION

JANUARY 28, 2014

Serial No. 113–48

Printed for the use of the Committee on Homeland Security

Available via the World Wide Web: http://www.gpo.gov/fdsys/

U.S. GOVERNMENT PRINTING OFFICE

87–973 PDF   WASHINGTON : 2014

For sale by the Superintendent of Documents, U.S. Government Printing Office
Internet: bookstore.gpo.gov   Phone: toll free (866) 512–1800; DC area (202) 512–1800
Fax: (202) 512–2250   Mail: Stop SSOP, Washington, DC 20402–0001

COMMITTEE ON HOMELAND SECURITY

MICHAEL T. MCCAUL, Texas, *Chairman*

LAMAR SMITH, Texas
PETER T. KING, New York
MIKE ROGERS, Alabama
PAUL C. BROUN, Georgia
CANDICE S. MILLER, Michigan, *Vice Chair*
PATRICK MEEHAN, Pennsylvania
JEFF DUNCAN, South Carolina
TOM MARINO, Pennsylvania
JASON CHAFFETZ, Utah
STEVEN M. PALAZZO, Mississippi
LOU BARLETTA, Pennsylvania
RICHARD HUDSON, North Carolina
STEVE DAINES, Montana
SUSAN W. BROOKS, Indiana
SCOTT PERRY, Pennsylvania
MARK SANFORD, South Carolina
VACANCY

BENNIE G. THOMPSON, Mississippi
LORETTA SANCHEZ, California
SHEILA JACKSON LEE, Texas
YVETTE D. CLARKE, New York
BRIAN HIGGINS, New York
CEDRIC L. RICHMOND, Louisiana
WILLIAM R. KEATING, Massachusetts
RON BARBER, Arizona
DONDALD M. PAYNE, JR., New Jersey
BETO O'ROURKE, Texas
TULSI GABBARD, Hawaii
FILEMON VELA, Texas
STEVEN A. HORSFORD, Nevada
ERIC SWALWELL, California

VACANCY, *Chief of Staff*
MICHAEL GEFFROY, *Deputy Chief of Staff / Chief Counsel*
MICHAEL S. TWINCHEK, *Chief Clerk*
I. LANIER AVANT, *Minority Staff Director*

SUBCOMMITTEE ON TRANSPORTATION SECURITY

RICHARD HUDSON, North Carolina, *Chairman*

MIKE ROGERS, Alabama, *Vice Chair*
CANDICE S. MILLER, Michigan
SUSAN W. BROOKS, Indiana
MARK SANFORD, South Carolina
MICHAEL T. MCCAUL, Texas *(ex officio)*

CEDRIC L. RICHMOND, Louisiana
SHEILA JACKSON LEE, Texas
ERIC SWALWELL, California
BENNIE G. THOMPSON, Mississippi *(ex officio)*

AMANDA PARIKH, *Subcommittee Staff Director*
DENNIS TERRY, *Subcommittee Clerk*
BRIAN TURBYFILL, *Minority Subcommittee Staff Director*

CONTENTS

STATEMENTS

WITNESSES

EXAMINING TSA'S CADRE OF CRIMINAL INVESTIGATORS

Tuesday, January 28, 2014

U.S. HOUSE OF REPRESENTATIVES,
SUBCOMMITTEE ON TRANSPORTATION SECURITY,
COMMITTEE ON HOMELAND SECURITY,
Washington, DC.

The subcommittee met, pursuant to call, at 1:29 p.m., in Room 311, Cannon House Office Building, Hon. Richard Hudson [Chairman of the subcommittee] presiding.

Present: Representatives Hudson, Rogers, Brooks, Sanford, and Richmond.

Mr. HUDSON. The Committee on Homeland Security Subcommittee on Transportation Security will come to order.

Subcommittee is meeting today to hear testimony examining TSA's workforce of criminal investigators and how TSA can improve the management of its Office of Inspection to ensure it is meeting requirements set forth by Federal law and regulations.

I recognize myself for an opening statement.

I would first like to thank our witnesses, not only for being here today but also for their public service. I appreciate their willingness to come forward and work on ways to solve the difficult issues the Transportation Security Administration faces.

The problem before us today is not a new one and it can, in fact, be traced back to the legislation that created the Transportation Security Administration 2 months after the terrorist attacks of 9/11.

The Aviation and Transportation Security Act, or ATSA, gave TSA sweeping authorities to, among other things, create its own employee classification system rather than adhere to the Office of Personnel Management system like the vast majority of other Federal agencies. At the time, Congress determined it was best to align TSA with the Federal Aviation Administration, which also has its own employee classification system separate and apart from OPM.

Today TSA has 20 percent more employees than FAA and we continue to see significant challenges with the size and scope of TSA's workforce—challenges that are likely exacerbated by TSA's exemption from the OPM system. Today's hearing is an opportunity to examine one glaring example of the problem.

TSA has roughly 100 employees in the Office of Inspection who are classified as criminal investigators. In order for these criminal investigators to receive premium law enforcement pay, TSA is required to confirm that they spend the majority of their time on long-term criminal investigations related to alleged or suspected violations of Federal criminal law.

The I.G.'s office found no evidence that TSA had actually done this, and yet these criminal investigators are still receiving premium pay. According to the I.G., TSA's criminal investigators spend the majority of their time investigating non-criminal cases, monitoring criminal cases conducted by other agencies, and carrying out inspections, covert tests, and internal reviews. Non-criminal investigators or other non-law enforcement employees could just as easily carry out the bulk of these tasks.

All these activities appear valuable, particularly the covert testing, so it is not my intent to disparage the hard work of these men and women. However, the I.G. estimates that if TSA does nothing to correct this situation of misclassification it will cost the taxpayers at least $17.5 million over the next 5 years in premium pay alone. That does not include other expenses such as law enforcement officer training, weapons, ammunition, vehicles, communications equipment, and enhanced retirement benefits.

What message does it send to the law enforcement officers who put their lives on the line every day to keep us safe or those who have lost their job due to budget cuts if TSA does not play by the same rules as other agencies? We are all accountable to the taxpayer and this subcommittee is responsible for holding TSA to standards the American people expect and deserve.

Today we have the assistant administrators for two offices in TSA with significant potential to fix this problem.

Mr. Allison, you have been in your position for a year and 4 months. In that time I understand you have tried to make some changes.

I hope you will share these today and provide us with suggestions of how we can resolve this problem. I look forward to hearing specifically how you intend to address all the I.G.'s recommendations.

Ms. Shelton Waters, it was not too long ago that you testified before this subcommittee as the head of TSA's acquisition office. As the head of the Office of Human Capital it is your duty to ensure that TSA is not abusing the unique authority it has been given to maintain its own employee classification system and to provide the Office of Inspection the tools and support it needs to make significant changes.

Finally, Ms. Richards, I look forward to hearing directly from you on the numerous recommendations put forth in your report and how we can bring greater accountability to TSA's Office of Inspection and shine a light on TSA's employee classification system.

Okay. When our Ranking Member gets here, Mr. Richmond, who we are anticipating will be here, I will recognize him for his opening statement. In the mean time, we are trying to move forward as quick as we can due to the vote schedule, and so at this point we will move right into witness testimony.

Other Members of the committee are reminded that opening statements may be submitted for the record.

[The statements of Ranking Member Richmond and Ranking Member Thompson follows:]

STATEMENT OF RANKING MEMBER CEDRIC L. RICHMOND

JANUARY 28, 2014

As you all know, the work that this subcommittee does is extremely important. We are tasked with making sure that the Transportation Security Administration fulfills its mission of protecting the Nation's transportation systems to ensure freedom of movement for people and commerce.

More importantly, we are tasked with ensuring the safety of American Citizens as they travel across the Nation.

To accomplish this mission, we must ensure that every office within the Transportation Security Administration is operating both effectively and efficiently.

The report released in September 2013 by the Department of Homeland Security's Office of Inspector General regarding the Office of Inspection is both alarming and scathing. The report details that the Office of Inspection is not operating at maximum efficiency, or in a cost-effective manner because of a top-heavy structure.

Specifically, the Office of Inspection employs personnel classified as "criminal investigators", despite their duties not fitting the classification of criminal investigations according to Federal regulations. This classification allows these "criminal investigators" to receive enhanced benefits, and LEAP pay.

According to the OIG report, and as I understand it, two prior reports, substantial savings could be achieved by reclassifying these "criminal investigators" in a manner consistent with the needs of the Office of Inspection and the type of work they perform.

Undoubtedly, there are many examples of instances in which the Office of Inspection has helped thwart the efforts of nefarious actors who mean to do our Nation harm.

That, however, does not diminish the need for us to use our resources effectively so that we can operate at maximum efficiency.

It is my hope that through the testimony we gather today, we can get further insight about where these inefficiencies are occurring, how we can reallocate our resources in an effective manner, and also what can be done structurally within the TSA so that when these structural problems are first brought to light, they can be quickly addressed.

I look forward to all of the witnesses' testimony, and hope that the work that we do here today aids in making the Transportation Security Administration stronger, more efficient, and more effective.

Before yielding back, I would like to note that this is the first hearing of the subcommittee in the Second Session of this Congress.

It is my expectation that this subcommittee will be as bipartisan and productive this year as it was last year when our subcommittee produced four out of the five bills that the committee saw pass the House.

I look forward to continuing to work with the Chairman to see that the bills we sent to the Senate in December, including Ranking Member Thompson's bill to codify the Aviation Security Advisory Committee, become law this year.

————

STATEMENT OF RANKING MEMBER BENNIE G. THOMPSON

JANUARY 28, 2014

Last September, the Department of Homeland Security's Office of Inspector General released a report that was highly critical of the way the Office of Inspection classifies its employees and documents its work.

The OIG report was not the first to identify inefficiencies within TSA's Office of Inspection. Indeed, it is the third such report in the last 3 years to come to the same conclusion. In 2011, TSA's Office of Human Capital conducted a position management review of the Office of Inspection and found that its workload did not support the number of criminal investigators in the office.

Following this review, the Office of Human Capital contracted with a private company to conduct a comprehensive position classification audit of the Office of Inspection. The result was the same; positions were found to have been misclassified.

The findings of a single report may be the result of anomalies or misunderstandings. Three consecutive reports conducted by distinct entities with the same conclusions cannot be so easily dismissed. Clearly, reforms within the Office of Inspection are in order.

I can assure you that if TSA does not act to see that the office is reorganized and made more efficient, this committee will take it upon itself to mandate the reforms needed. When Congress established TSA in 2001, it gave the agency broad authority to set its personnel practices as it saw fit to best accomplish its critical mission. With that authority comes a great deal of responsibility.

Unfortunately, it appears TSA's Office of Inspection has not been a responsible steward of its authority to classify positions. As a result, the office has more employees designated as criminal investigators than any independent audit shows they need. This dynamic has resulted in increased cost to taxpayers and less efficiency within a critical component of TSA.

To the witnesses here today from TSA, Mr. Allison and Ms. Shelton Waters, I look forward to hearing from you about the steps you intend to take to address the findings and recommendations in the Inspector General's report.

Beyond the concerns I have about classification of employees within the Office of Inspection, I am gravely concerned by the Inspector General's finding that management at TSA may not be able to rely on the office's work.

As Assistant Administrator Allison's written testimony points out, the Office of Inspection's mission is to ensure the integrity, efficiency, and effectiveness of TSA's workforce, operations, and programs.

If structural and organizational flaws within the Office of Inspection compromise its ability to perform its mission, the entire agency suffers.

If those same deficiencies result in the administrator not being able to rely on the office's work, we have a much bigger problem on our hands.

Both the administrator and the workforce must have confidence that the Office of Inspection is an efficient and effective entity that holds itself to the highest possible standard. The Inspector General's report calls that into question.

To all of the witnesses appearing before us today, I thank you for appearing and for your service. It is my hope that today's hearing will allow for a productive dialog whereby solutions to the problems that have plagued the Office of Inspection since long before Assistant Administrator Allison took over responsibility for the office can be identified.

Mr. HUDSON. We are very pleased to have a distinguished panel of witnesses with us today.

Mr. Roderick Allison is TSA's assistant administrator for inspection at the Transportation Security Administration, a position he has held since August 2012. In this capacity Mr. Allison oversees and ensures the security and integrity of TSA's operations through inspections, investigations, and covert testing. Before becoming assistant administrator Mr. Allison served as the deputy assistant administrator and deputy director for the Office of Law Enforcement within the Federal Air Marshal Service.

Ms. Karen Shelton Waters is TSA's assistant administrator for human capital. Ms. Shelton Waters is responsible for programs that empower TSA to hire, retain, and deploy a qualified workforce. Previously, Ms. Shelton Waters served as TSA's assistant administrator for the Office of Acquisition.

Finally, Ms. Anne Richards is the assistant inspector general for the Office of Audits under the Office of Inspector General at the Department of Homeland Security. The Office of Audits focuses on promoting effectiveness, efficiency, and economy in DHS's programs and operations in addition to detecting fraud, abuse, waste, and mismanagement. Prior to joining the Office of Inspector General Ms. Richards was assistant inspector general at the U.S. Department of the Interior.

The witnesses' full statements will appear in the record.

The Chairman now recognizes Mr. Allison to testify.

STATEMENT OF RODERICK ALLISON, ASSISTANT ADMINISTRATOR, OFFICE OF INSPECTION, TRANSPORTATION SECURITY ADMINISTRATION, U.S. DEPARTMENT OF HOMELAND SECURITY

Mr. ALLISON. Thank you, Mr. Chairman.

Chairman Hudson, Ranking Member Richmond, and Members of the subcommittee, I appreciate the opportunity to appear before you today. As the Chairman said, my name is Roderick Allison; I am the assistant administrator for the Office of Inspection, or OOI.

The TSA administrator and deputy administrator have stated that TSA has zero tolerance for misconduct. In fact, in July of last year the deputy administrator testified before your subcommittee and the Subcommittee on Oversight and Management Efficiency on TSA's role in promoting a strong counterterrorism workforce to safeguard the traveling public and secure our Nation's transportation systems. In that testimony the deputy administrator highlighted OOI's role and responsibilities to investigate misconduct by TSA employees.

One of TSA's mission priorities is efficiencies and the administrator has charged his staff to find efficiencies in our respective organizations. To that point, beginning in fiscal year 2013 OOI initiated and completed more organizational improvements in that year than the previous 5 years combined.

OOI is responsible for investigations, audits, and compliance inspections, as well as covert testing efforts. We investigate allegations of criminal and administrative misconduct by TSA employees and contractors, conduct inspections of TSA through covert testing and audits designed to identify system vulnerabilities and provide mitigation strategies.

In 2013 we conducted over 400 covert tests at 136 airports, and through our September 11 security fee audits we identified over $753,000 in fees due back to TSA—or back to the Government. Since 2008 our audit program has identified over $13 million in security fees owed back to TSA.

In fiscal year 2013 OOI closed 887 investigations, an 11 percent increase in productivity over the previous year, with approximately 55 percent of selected cases closed within 90 days. Also in fiscal year 2013 OOI opened 747 criminal administrative conduct miscases. This number includes 423 cases that TSA was required to refer to the DHS OIG, which they retained only 3 percent of the 423 cases and referred the remaining back to TSA for investigations.

Additionally, our investigators completed 25 Office of Worker's Compensation fraud investigations, OWCP, which have resulted in $3 million in cost avoidance to the Government. In total, our OWCP investigations have resulted in saving the taxpayers $57 million in fraudulent claims.

In fiscal year 2013 OOI criminal investigators also provided technical service to our investigations, including 113 criminal polygraph examinations, 137 computer forensic analyses, and 135 technical equipment support services. In 2012, at the request of Administrator Pistole, our office initiated theft stings, or what we call integrity testing.

During 2013 fiscal year, we conducted over 2,500 tests at 114 airports around the country. I am pleased to announce that in that effort we have a 99.7 percent pass rate, and the employees that we caught were removed from Federal service.

The administrator office routinely publishes the results of these tests and broadcasts e-mails and newsletters to the workforce on this effort and we intend to continue. All these milestones were achieved with a 6 percent reduction in the number of criminal investigators during the fiscal year.

In September 2013 DHS OIG report on Office of Inspection, which is the subject of today's hearing, offered 11 recommendations and we have concurred with each of them. These recommendations will further refine and improve the performance of the Office of Inspection.

For example, recommendation No. 5 focused on developing an annual work plan, and recommendations No. 6 and 7 center on developing and tracking outcome-based performance measures. Recommendation No. 8, which we have already undertaken, required employees, including criminal investigators, to document their work hours to investigations and other assignments in an automated system.

In fact, on December 20, 2013 we submitted documentation to OIG to request closure of the 10 remaining open recommendations and the OIG is currently evaluating our documentation.

While we have concurred with each of the OIG recommendations, I believe that the independent workforce analysis outlined in recommendation No. 3, along with the data we are now completely tracking, will provide TSA with the necessary information to determine what the proper number of investigative positions—or what positions TSA should have with respect to that number, I am sorry. As noted in our 90-day response to the report, we expect that analysis and classification review to be completed by September.

In closing, it is our responsibility to conduct impartial, thorough, and expedient investigations of misconduct to uphold the integrity of our workforce. However, we are also responsible for ensuring that allegations of misconduct do not compromise TSA's ability to perform its security mission.

It is important to note that while our investigations often substantiate allegations of wrongdoing, many cases exonerate employees of allegations of misconduct. Effectively managing these cases in a time frame consonant with the allegations allow these employees to return to their security duties.

I appreciate the opportunity to appear before you today, and I will be happy to answer any questions you may have.

[The joint prepared statement of Mr. Allison and Ms. Waters follows:]

JOINT PREPARED STATEMENT OF RODERICK ALLISON AND KAREN SHELTON WATERS

JANUARY 28, 2014

Chairman Hudson, Ranking Member Richmond, and Members of the subcommittee, I appreciate the opportunity to appear before you to discuss the Transportation Security Administration's (TSA) Office of Inspection (OOI). I am joined today by Karen Shelton Waters, TSA's assistant administrator for the Office of Human Capital.

TSA OOI ensures the integrity and effectiveness of TSA's employees and programs, which are entrusted with safeguarding our Nation's transportation systems, as well as the security systems used to safeguard the traveling public.

TSA OOI's mission is to ensure the integrity, efficiency, and effectiveness of TSA's workforce, operations, and programs through objective audits, covert testing, inspections, and criminal investigations. Every day, TSA's nearly 60,000 employees screen 1.8 million air travelers, and perform the vetting for more than 2 million new airline passenger reservations and 14 million transportation worker records against the

Federal Government's consolidated terrorist watch list. It is critical to our mission that the TSA workforce and its programs adhere to the highest standards of conduct.

TSA'S OFFICE OF INSPECTION

TSA OOI has a wide range of responsibilities including criminal investigations, audit and compliance cases, as well as covert testing efforts. We investigate allegations of criminal and administrative misconduct of TSA employees and contractors; conduct inspections of TSA operations to ensure all offices and airports are in full compliance with Federal laws, regulations, and current policies; and evaluate the effectiveness of our transportation security systems through covert testing and audits designed to identify system vulnerabilities and provide mitigation strategies. Of these, there are 100 criminal investigators who handle allegations of criminal and administrative misconduct. The criminal investigators have an average of 17 years of Federal experience, including an average of 7 years of service at TSA.

In 2012, at Administrator Pistole's direction, TSA OOI initiated integrity tests at airports around the country to assess compliance with our core value of integrity in handling the property of passengers. Since 2012, TSA OOI's criminal investigators have conducted more than 2,530 integrity tests in 114 airports around the country. At times, the tests included local law enforcement and Department of Homeland Security (DHS) Office of Inspector General (OIG), Office of Investigations agents. I am pleased to report that we have found 99.7 percent compliance. In fact, only 7 TSA employees failed the covert tests and all 7 were removed from Federal service.

TSA is required by DHS Management Directive 0810.1 to refer allegations of criminal misconduct to the DHS OIG, so the DHS OIG may determine which cases it will retain and investigate. Any case DHS OIG does not choose to investigate is referred back to TSA OOI. This responsibility requires the employment and retention of investigators who are professional, capable, and able to appropriately handle criminal investigation cases. In fiscal year 2013, TSA referred 423 new cases to the DHS OIG, which retained 12 cases. The remaining 411 cases were referred back to TSA OOI for investigation.

EFFICIENCY

During fiscal year 2013, TSA OOI's 100 criminal investigators completed 887[1] total investigations including 309 of the 411 newly-opened cases referenced above, of which the majority were criminal investigations. TSA OOI's criminal investigators used their expertise and knowledge of law, regulation, and policy to investigate and close these complex cases, thus ensuring the highest standards of integrity and professionalism within our workforce. Additionally, TSA OOI partners with the TSA Office of Professional Responsibility (OPR) to ensure that allegations of misconduct are thoroughly investigated and that discipline is appropriate, consistent, and fair across the agency.

Since becoming the assistant administrator of TSA OOI, I have focused on making our office more efficient and effective in carrying out its mission. During fiscal year 2013, TSA OOI closed over 55 percent of investigations within 90 days of initiation. In fiscal year 2013, TSA OOI completed 25 workers' compensation fraud investigations which resulted in cost avoidance to the Government of over $3,000,000. Our office also conducted over 400 covert tests, which focused on potential vulnerabilities in existing policies, procedures, supervision, and training. Furthermore, OOI implemented risk-based initiatives through the development and implementation of tools, conducted risk-based analysis of information for program development and execution, and collaborated with internal and external stakeholders.

OIG RECOMMENDATIONS

The OIG produced a September 2013 report entitled *Transportation Security Administration Office of Inspection's Efforts to Enhance Transportation Security* which recommended 11 improvements in TSA OOI. While the majority of these recommendations are still open, TSA has made a significant progress in addressing the OIG's concerns such as Recommendation No. 2, which the OIG closed when TSA finalized and implemented a Management Directive requiring criminal investigators to document their work hours properly. To adequately capture the utilization of our criminal investigators, TSA OOI uses a Resource Allocation Model (RAM) to docu-

---

[1] The 887 completed investigations include new cases from fiscal year 2013 as well as cases opened or investigated in the prior year.

ment all criminal investigative activities and hours concurrent with the investigation, which supervisors are reviewing on a regular basis.

Additionally, TSA's Office of Human Capital (OHC) is conducting an independent workforce review to evaluate the workforce profile and the nature of the caseload in TSA OOI. This will ensure the proper assignment of cases requiring the special skills and expertise of criminal investigators. The evaluation will also include a predictive model to determine the future demand for criminal investigators. As part of this review, OHC will examine cost-effective and appropriate staffing models to support TSA OOI's mission.

On December 9, 2013, I approved a work plan for TSA OOI's divisions, which contains project-specific information such as duration, cost estimates, and staffing. I am also reviewing our current fiscal year goals to develop outcome-based performance measures, and working to establish a regular review process to ensure that TSA OOI's programs, projects, and operations are meeting the intended goals. TSA OOI anticipates completing this task in March of this year.

TSA produced a 90-day update to the OIG's recommendations in December of 2013, and anticipates closure of additional recommendations in the coming weeks.

CONCLUSION

TSA appreciates the partnership of the DHS OIG and this committee to ensure TSA OOI is managing our security system and workforce in the most efficient, effective manner possible. Thank you for the opportunity to appear before you today. I will be happy to address any questions you may have.

Mr. HUDSON. Thank you, Mr. Allison.

The Chairman recognizes Ms. Shelton Waters to testify.

STATEMENT OF KAREN SHELTON WATERS, ASSISTANT ADMINISTRATOR, OFFICE OF HUMAN CAPITAL, TRANSPORTATION SECURITY ADMINISTRATION, U.S. DEPARTMENT OF HOMELAND SECURITY

Ms. SHELTON WATERS. Good afternoon, Chairman Hudson, Ranking Member Richmond, and Members of the subcommittee. My name is Karen Shelton Waters and I am the assistant administrator for the Office of Human Capital at the Transportation Security Administration.

In my position I serve as the principal agency adviser on matters pertaining to human capital. Among other things, my office is responsible for providing human capital services to develop and sustain a high-performing workforce, developing the agency's human capital policy agenda, and monitoring progress towards those goals, implementing survey systems to gauge organizational effectiveness and workforce job satisfaction, ensuring sound position management principles are in place throughout TSA, and ensuring the TSA personnel management system supports legislative and policy requirements such as merit principles, prohibited personnel practices, diversity in hiring, and application of veterans preference.

Through each of these functions, Human Capital supports TSA's program offices in meeting their mission needs. For example, when the agency needs to hire a canine handler or a Federal air marshal it is the program office that provides the technical skills and ability required for the position. Human Capital assists the program office by reviewing and advising on the proper classification of the position, creating the vacancy announcement, advising on recruitments strategy, and evaluating the applicants. The list of qualified applicants is then provided to the hiring office for review and selection.

TSA is somewhat unique in that it is an excepted service agency. TSA's human capital authorities are outlined by the Aviation and Transportation Security Act and not Title 5 of the U.S. Code.

The act provided that, among other things, the TSA administrator develop a personnel system that, at a minimum, provided for greater flexibility in hiring, training, compensation, and location of personnel. TSA's core compensation does this.

It is also important to note that the Office of Personnel Management has approved an interchange agreement with DHS for TSA after determining TSA's established merit system is consistent with the intent of civil service laws.

As you know, Administrator Pistole and the TSA leadership are committed to the culture of hard work, professionalism, and integrity. In furtherance of those ideals, the agency has taken a number of steps in recent years, including the creation of the Office of Professional Responsibility, or OPR.

OPR works closely in conjunction with the Office of Inspection to ensure that allegations of misconduct are swiftly and thoroughly investigated and that misconduct is dealt with consistently and appropriately. My role in that process is to ensure that my colleagues in Inspection and OPR have the necessary staffing and resources to achieve those results.

With respect to the Inspector General report being discussed here today, I will have an independent analysis of the criminal investigator workforce conducted and then use the results of that analysis to assist OOI in balancing their criminal investigator workforce against the agency's criminal investigative workload. I am committed to work with the Office of Inspection and the TSA leadership to utilize cost-effective human capital processes and practices that provide the appropriate resources needed to ensure the integrity of the TSA workforce.

Thank you for the opportunity to appear before you today. I will be happy to answer any questions you may have.

Mr. HUDSON. Thank you, Ms. Shelton Waters.

The Chairman recognizes Ms. Richards to testify.

STATEMENT OF ANNE L. RICHARDS, ASSISTANT INSPECTOR GENERAL, OFFICE OF AUDITS, U.S. DEPARTMENT OF HOMELAND SECURITY

Ms. RICHARDS. Good afternoon, Chairman Hudson, Ranking Member Richmond, Members of the subcommittee. Thank you for inviting me to testify on our recent audit of TSA's Office of Inspection.

During our audit we identified several issues that led us to conclude the Office of Inspection was not operating efficiently or effectively. Specifically, we determined that using criminal investigators to conduct inspections, covert testing, and internal reviews was not cost-effective because other employees who are paid less could perform the same work.

We also concluded that more than 100 Office of Inspection staff members who were classified as criminal investigators may not have met Federal requirements entitling them to extra pay, called law enforcement ability pay, or LEAP. To receive LEAP, criminal investigators must spend, on average, at least 50 percent of their time on criminal investigations, that is investigating, apprehending, or detaining individuals suspected or convicted of criminal offenses.

The office's criminal investigators worked primarily on collateral and administrative cases rather than on criminal cases. Data compiled by our Office of Investigations indicated that in fiscal years 2010 and 2011 about 75 percent of the Office of Inspection's workload consisted of collateral and administrative cases. This means that criminal investigators primarily monitored and reported on criminal investigations conducted by other agencies or investigated cases of alleged employee misconduct.

During our audit period Office of Inspection employees, including criminal investigators, were not required to document their activities so the office could not definitively show that its criminal investigators met the LEAP requirements. Yet, 97 percent received LEAP.

We estimate that if the office maintains the same number of criminal investigator positions the cost of LEAP over the next 5 years will add up to $17.5 million, most of which could be avoided if the workload analysis was performed and its recommendations promptly implemented. This estimate does not include the cost of special employment benefits for law enforcement officers or additional costs in training, travel, and supplies.

For these reasons we recommended that a workforce analysis and a position classification review be performed for the Office of Inspection. We believe that OPM would be best suited to conduct this work independently and objectively.

TSA has reported that the Office of Inspection is working with the Office of Human Capital on a workforce analysis, but the review will cover only two divisions which employ just 12 of the current 105 criminal investigators in the office. There were no plans to review the other 87 criminal investigator positions. This is troubling because a previous study by the Office of Human Capital and by a contractor hired by the Office of Human Capital identified similar issues as our audit work, but those recommendations were not accepted or implemented.

Our audit also showed that the office did not effectively plan its work, did not adequately measure its performance, and did not ensure that all divisions complied with the professional standards it had committed to using. The office also could not ensure that staff members were properly trained and that supervisors adequately reviewed work products.

Without proper quality controls, TSA could not be certain that Office of Inspection's work was reliable. In addition, TSA was not obligated to implement the office's recommendations and therefore may have missed opportunities to improve transportation security.

Mr. Chairman, this concludes my remarks. Thank you.

[The prepared statement of Ms. Richards follows:]

PREPARED STATEMENT OF ANNE L. RICHARDS

JANUARY 28, 2014

Good afternoon Chairman Hudson, Ranking Member Richmond, and Members of the subcommittee.

Thank you for inviting me here today to testify on the Transportation Security Administration (TSA) Office of Inspection's (OOI) efforts to enhance transportation security. My testimony will focus on the results of our audit to determine the efficiency and effectiveness of OOI's efforts, which we published in September 2013.

OOI conducts inspections, internal reviews, and covert testing to ensure the effectiveness and efficiency of TSA's operations and administrative activities, and to identify vulnerabilities in TSA security systems. Additionally, the office carries out internal investigations of the TSA workforce to ensure its integrity. We conducted an audit of this office to determine whether it is efficient and effective in its efforts to enhance transportation security.

We determined that OOI did not operate efficiently. Specifically, the office did not use its staff and resources efficiently to conduct cost-effective inspections, internal reviews, and covert testing. OOI employed personnel classified as criminal investigators, even though their primary duties may not have been criminal investigations as required by Federal law and regulations. These employees received premium pay and other costly benefits, although other employees were able to perform the same work at a lower cost. Additionally, the office did not properly plan its work and resource needs, track project costs, or measure performance effectively. Quality controls were not sufficient to ensure that inspections, internal reviews, and covert testing complied with accepted standards; that staff members were properly trained; and that work was adequately reviewed. Finally, the office could not always ensure that other TSA offices acted on its recommendations to improve operations.

As a result of these issues with the office's cost-effectiveness and quality controls over its work products, TSA was not as effective as it could have been, and management may not be able to rely on the office's work. Additionally, OOI may not have fully accomplished its mission to identify and address transportation security vulnerabilities. With the appropriate classification and training of staff and better use of resources, the office could improve the quality of its work. The appropriate number of reclassifications and more precise cost savings cannot be determined without an objective and comprehensive review of position classifications. If TSA does not make any changes to the number of criminal investigator positions in OOI, we estimate that it will cost as much as $17.5 million over 5 years for premium Law Enforcement Availability Pay (LEAP). OOI could realize further savings in training, travel, supplies, and other special employment benefits, including statutory early retirement, if its personnel classified as criminal investigators were reclassified to non-criminal investigator positions.

BACKGROUND

TSA is responsible for protecting the Nation's transportation systems. The agency provides airline and other transportation security through passenger, baggage, and container screening, as well as other security programs. OOI's mission is to: (1) Ensure the effectiveness and efficiency of TSA's operations and administrative activities through inspections and internal reviews, (2) identify vulnerabilities in security systems through operational testing, and (3) ensure the integrity of TSA's workforce through comprehensive special investigations. At the time of our audit, OOI was composed of the following four divisions:

- *Inspections and Investigations Division.*—Inspects TSA program components, including the Federal Air Marshal Service, Federal Security Directors' offices, and TSA Headquarters' offices to ensure they are following TSA's policies and procedures. Additionally, the division identifies vulnerabilities in passenger, baggage, and cargo operations; it also investigates alleged criminal and administrative misconduct of TSA employees.
- *Internal Reviews Division.*—Assesses TSA programs and operations for efficiency, effectiveness, and compliance with laws, regulations, and TSA policies. The division also conducts audits of air carriers in accordance with *Government Auditing Standards*, to determine their compliance with 9/11 security fee requirements. From 2008 through 2011, the division audited approximately $4.8 billion in 9/11 security fees and identified approximately $12.6 million in fees that were owed to the Federal Government.
- *Special Operations Division.*—Plans, conducts, and reports results of covert testing to identify vulnerabilities in transportation security systems. Covert testing is designed to identify security vulnerabilities and address deficiencies by recommending corrective actions.
- *Business Management Office.*—Supports the three operational divisions by managing OOI's communications and information systems and coordinating resources.

As shown in Table 1, OOI reported the following accomplishments from fiscal year 2010 through the first quarter of fiscal year 2012.

TABLE 1.—INVESTIGATIONS OPENED AND REPORTS COMPLETED FROM
FISCAL YEAR 2010 THROUGH FIRST QUARTER FISCAL YEAR 2012

	Amount
Investigations Opened	930
Reports of Inspections	93
Reports of Internal Reviews	56
Reports of Special Operations (Covert Testing)	16

Source.—Totals based on data provided by OOI.

In fiscal year 2011, the TSA Office of Human Capital (OHC) conducted a position management review in OOI and reported that the office could gain efficiencies by restructuring its organization, realigning its workload, reclassifying positions, and refocusing on core functions and purpose.[1] In fiscal year 2012, at the direction of the TSA administrator, OHC began an Organizational Transformation Initiative. The initiative is designed to support the agency's on-going evolution into a high-performance counterterrorism organization and ensure that each TSA office executes its assigned responsibilities efficiently, effectively, and economically. As a result, OOI changed its organizational structure and, in an effort to reduce the number of supervisory layers, eliminated several positions.

OOI staff is composed primarily of personnel employed in positions classified by TSA as criminal investigators, transportation security specialists, and program analysts who operate in a matrix environment in which individuals assist divisions other than the one to which they are assigned. For example, in addition to conducting investigations, criminal investigators may conduct inspections or covert testing. According to data provided by OOI's Business Management Office, in fiscal year 2011, TSA allocated approximately $43.5 million to OOI, of which $27.2 million was spent on salaries for 205 employees, including 35 transportation security specialists and 124 criminal investigators. Transportation security specialists supervise, lead, or perform inspections, investigations, enforcement, or compliance work. TSA defines a criminal investigator as an individual who plans and conducts investigations of alleged or suspected violations of Federal criminal laws.

According to TSA Management Directive No. 1100.88–1, *Law Enforcement Position Standards and Hiring Requirements*, TSA criminal investigators are considered law enforcement officers. By law, however, to qualify for statutory enhanced retirement benefits, only those Federal employees whose duties include "primarily the investigation, apprehension, or detention of individuals suspected or convicted of offenses against the criminal laws of the United States" qualify as law enforcement officers.[2] Office of Personnel Management (OPM) regulations require law enforcement officers to spend in general an average of at least 50 percent of their time investigating, apprehending, or detaining individuals suspected or convicted of violating criminal laws of the United States.[3]

Law enforcement officers are entitled to special statutory employment benefits. For example, they are entitled to retire at age 50 with full benefits after 20 years of service.[4] They receive a faster accruing pension. They also are eligible to receive extra pay known as LEAP.[5] Although TSA is exempt from certain personnel management provisions of Title V of the United States Code (USC), including the LEAP statute, TSA Management Directive No. 1100.88–1 incorporates LEAP.[6] To receive LEAP, an additional 25 percent above base pay, criminal investigators must certify annually that they have worked and are expected to be available to work a min-

[1] *TSA OHC Position Management Review, Office of Inspection*, August 2011.

[2] 5 United States Code (USC) §8331(20), §8401(17), 5 Code of Federal Regulations (CFR). §831.902; see also 5 CFR. §842.802.

[3] 5 CFR §§831.902, 842.802. These regulations define and establish requirements for law enforcement officers. This workload requirement does not apply to individuals who qualify to be in a secondary position, such as first-level supervisors to criminal investigators or those in administrative positions.

[4] 5 USC §§8336(c), 8412(d)(2).

[5] Congress enacted the *Law Enforcement Availability Pay Act of 1994* "to provide premium pay to criminal investigators to ensure the availability of criminal investigators for unscheduled duty in excess of a 40-hour work week based on the needs of the employing agency." 5 USC §5545a(b).

[6] TSA's Management Directive No. 1100.88–1 also incorporates the statutory and regulatory definitions of "law enforcement officer" referred to throughout this report. TSA is not exempt from Title V provisions concerning law enforcement retirement.

imum annual average of 2 or more unscheduled duty hours beyond each normal workday.[7]

Because of their position classifications, OOI criminal investigators are eligible for LEAP and entitled to early retirement. These benefits are more costly to the Government than regular benefits.[8] Approximately 97 percent of OOI's criminal investigators received LEAP during the period of our audit. The salary for criminal investigators is capped and varies based on the differing locality pay of each duty station. For example, criminal investigators based in OOI headquarters in the Washington, DC, area have a salary cap of approximately $164,000, which includes LEAP and locality pay. From financial information we obtained from TSA, we determined that in fiscal year 2011, the median pay for an OOI criminal investigator was $161,794 and the median pay for a transportation security specialist was $117,775. TSA's records showed that in fiscal year 2011, salaries for criminal investigators, who comprised about 60 percent of OOI staff, accounted for $18.5 million, or 68 percent, of the $27.2 million in total salaries paid. OOI also paid criminal investigators approximately $6.1 million in LEAP over fiscal years 2010 and 2011. For purposes of this audit, we did not review the cost to TSA of other statutory law enforcement benefits such as early retirement. Chart 1 shows the total salaries paid by position in OOI for fiscal year 2011.

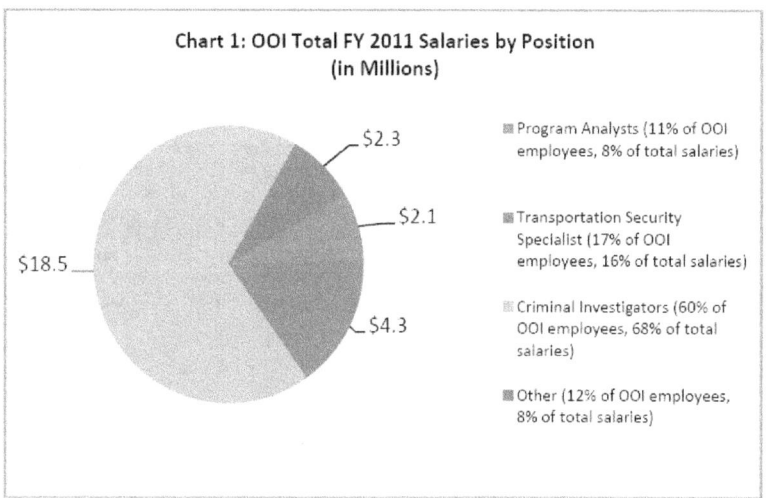

Chart 1: OOI Total FY 2011 Salaries by Position (in Millions)

- Program Analysts (11% of OOI employees, 8% of total salaries)
- Transportation Security Specialist (17% of OOI employees, 16% of total salaries)
- Criminal Investigators (60% of OOI employees, 68% of total salaries)
- Other (12% of OOI employees, 8% of total salaries)

$2.3 $2.1 $18.5 $4.3

Source: OIG generated based on data provided by OOI's Business Management Office.

In April 2012, the Department of Homeland Security (DHS) Office of Inspector General (OIG) Office of Investigations issued a *Report of Inspection for TSA's Office of Inspection, Inspections and Investigations Division* on OOI's process of conducting investigations into TSA employee misconduct. As a result of its inspection, the Office of Investigations determined that the Inspections and Investigations Division's investigative process complied with applicable policies, directives, and law enforcement standards. Because the Office of Investigations recently reviewed this process, we focused our audit on OOI's other products, services, and operations, and on personnel matters.

USE OF CRIMINAL INVESTIGATORS

OOI did not use its staff and resources efficiently in carrying out its work. The office did not have a process to ensure that its criminal investigators met their posi-

[7] *See* 5 CFR §§ 550.181–186, particularly § 550.184, Annual certification. Each newly hired criminal investigator and the appropriate supervisory officer must certify the investigator is expected to meet the substantial hours requirement in § 550.183 during the upcoming 1-year period. 5 CFR § 550.184(a).

[8] Eligibility for law enforcement retirement coverage must be "strictly construed" because the benefits are "more costly to the government than more traditional retirement plans and often results in the retirement of important people at a time when they would otherwise have continued to work for a number of years." *Bingaman* v. *Department of the Treasury*, 127 F.3d 1431, 1435 (Fed. Cir. 1997).

tions' criminal investigative workload requirement or were properly classified as criminal investigators. Rather than investigating criminal cases, the majority of the criminal investigators' workload consisted of noncriminal cases; monitoring and reporting on criminal cases; and carrying out inspections, covert testing, and internal reviews. Such work could have been performed by other OOI employees who do not receive LEAP, and who are not eligible for statutory early retirement and other costly law enforcement benefits.

OOI did not ensure that its criminal investigators met the Federal workload requirement for law enforcement officers, which makes them eligible for LEAP (if they meet the unscheduled hours availability requirement) and entitles them to early retirement. Specifically, the office could not ensure that its criminal investigators spent an average of at least 50 percent of their time investigating, apprehending, or detaining individuals suspected or convicted of criminal offenses. Additionally, some supervisory criminal investigators may not have been properly classified. Their classification depends on correctly classifying the individuals they supervise, and OOI had no assurance that subordinates were properly classified, based on the Federal workload requirement for criminal investigators. Although not able to demonstrate that criminal investigators met the Federal workload requirement for law enforcement officers, which is a prerequisite for receiving LEAP, OOI personnel in these positions and their supervisors received LEAP during the period of our audit.

DHS Management Directive 0810.1, *The Office of Inspector General*, requires OOI to refer allegations of potentially criminal employee misconduct to the DHS OIG Office of Investigations for review. Any case not retained by OIG is referred back to OOI. According to the April 2012 Office of Investigations report, OOI closed 1,125 cases in fical years 2010 and 2011; of the cases it closed, 253, or approximately 22.5 percent, were criminal in nature.

OOI criminal investigators primarily monitored and reported to TSA management the results of collateral criminal investigations conducted by other Federal, State, or local agencies, or they investigated administrative cases of alleged employee violations of TSA policy. Table 2 shows the Office of Investigations' categorization of 1,125 investigative cases closed by OOI in fiscal years 2010 and 2011. The statistics in Table 2 are based on the number of cases managed, not the time spent working on cases. Thus, these statistics do not address the Federal workload requirement for criminal investigators, which is based on time spent working on criminal investigations.

TABLE 2.—FISCAL YEAR 2010 AND FISCAL YEAR 2011 CLOSED CASE CATEGORIZATION

Type of Case	Category Description	Number	Percent of Total
Collateral	Criminal investigations conducted by other Federal, State, or local agencies, which OOI monitored and reported the results or investigated administratively.	577	51.3
Administrative	Investigations of TSA employee misconduct that violated TSA policy	295	26.2
Criminal (other than collateral)	Criminal investigations submitted for acceptance or declination to a U.S. attorney or State or local prosecutor when appropriate.	253	22.5
Total Cases	....	1,125	100

Source.—DHS OIG *Report of Inspection for TSA's Office of Inspection, Inspections and Investigations Division,* April 19, 2012.

In its 2011 position management review of OOI, OHC concluded that OOI's investigative workload did not support the number of criminal investigators in the office. According to a fiscal year 2011 OOI workload assessment, criminal investigators spent, in 1 year, an estimated 25 to 30 percent of their time on all investigations-related activities, whether monitoring collateral cases or conducting administrative and criminal investigations. Based on the OOI workload assessment, OHC raised concerns in its review about the number of criminal investigators in the Inspections and Investigations Division. In its report, OHC also noted that TSA is focused on transportation security and has a limited law enforcement function; therefore, modeling OOI after a law enforcement agency might not be appropriate.

As a result of its review, OHC concluded that OOI could improve its efficiency, and recommended that the office eliminate criminal investigator positions not supported by the criminal investigative workload, either through attrition or reassignment to an appropriate position. Following its position review, OHC contracted with a company to conduct comprehensive position classification audits of some OOI positions. These audits, the findings of which were presented to OHC in February 2012, confirmed OHC's findings that positions were misclassified.

Subsequently, OHC reversed its position, and no longer concurred with the contractor's findings regarding reclassifications. In its *Summary of Classification Determinations* dated June 2012, OHC maintained that these position classifications were secondary law enforcement positions, and as such there was "no required percentage of time or workload level required to sustain their classification as law enforcement." As of August 2012, OHC had not taken action to reevaluate and reclassify criminal investigator positions. Although OHC concluded in 2011 that OOI's investigative workload did not support the number of criminal investigators and recommended eliminating positions, in December 2012, OOI posted multiple vacancy announcements to hire more criminal investigators Nation-wide.

In June 2012, in response to OHC's position management review findings, the OOI assistant administrator at the time agreed to consult with OHC to assess the office's needs and determine the appropriate positions to perform OOI's work. The former assistant administrator also agreed to begin tracking criminal investigators' workload statistics to ensure that they met the legal requirement to spend a minimum of 50 percent of their time on criminal investigative activity. OOI Letter No. 0007.2, dated August 2012, requires its employees to track work hours, including LEAP hours, in its data management system.

OOI criminal investigators were also assigned to inspections, covert tests, and internal reviews, all of which could be accomplished by other personnel who do not receive LEAP or other statutory law enforcement benefits. Our review of 29 reports that were issued between fiscal year 2010 and the first quarter of fiscal year 2012 by various OOI divisions showed that criminal investigators composed:

- 61 percent of OOI personnel who conducted the 5 inspections;
- 50 percent of OOI personnel who conducted the 10 covert testing modules; and
- 51 percent of OOI personnel who conducted the 14 internal reviews.

These results show that criminal investigators performed work not related to criminal investigations, which is not an efficient use of resources. Paying LEAP to these employees costs more, and because they are not required to document the hours they spend conducting criminal investigations, it does not comply with TSA Management Directive 1100.88–1, which incorporates the LEAP statute. Using criminal investigators to perform this work also cost TSA more in salary and benefits.

OOI did not require all staff to enter time spent working on projects into its database, which would have supported the hours charged to its criminal investigations. Additionally, TSA has no assurance that the LEAP availability hours were properly certified because it was unable to determine whether the criminal investigators met the Federal workload requirement for that position. Without evidence to support the classification and workload of the 124 criminal investigators in OOI, there is no assurance that these positions are properly classified.

Using non-criminal investigators who do not receive LEAP to perform inspections, covert tests, and internal reviews could result in future cost savings. Specifically, we estimate that over a 5-year period, OOI could save as much as $17.5 million in LEAP if its 124 criminal investigators were reclassified to non-criminal investigator positions. However, the appropriate number of reclassifications and more precise cost savings cannot be determined without an objective and comprehensive review of position classifications.

Our cost savings estimate does not take into account a potential increase in overtime pay, which could result from criminal investigators being converted to transportation security specialists or program analysts. Criminal investigators who receive LEAP are not generally eligible to receive overtime pay, but transportation security specialists and program analysts are eligible.[9] During fiscal years 2010 and 2011, OOI paid approximately $109,000 in overtime pay to 66 individuals in these two job positions. If all 124 criminal investigators (approximately twice the number of OOI's transportation security specialists and program analysts who received overtime pay during this 2-year period) were converted, we estimate the increase in overtime pay would be approximately $218,000 based on pay data from fiscal years 2010 and 2011. This potential increase in overtime pay is significantly less than the $6.1 million paid in LEAP for the same 2-year period.

In addition to the LEAP savings, OOI could realize savings if its criminal investigators were reclassified as transportation security specialists or other non-criminal investigator positions. These savings would come from cost categories such as training, travel, supplies, and other benefits, including statutory early retirement and a faster-accruing pension. OHC reached this same conclusion in its position management review.

When OOI was established in September 2003, TSA management may have believed that the number of criminal investigators on staff was appropriate to meet the office's mission. However, in the 10 years since its establishment, neither OOI nor TSA has conducted a comprehensive workforce analysis, which would help determine the correct set of skills and the appropriate number of personnel to accomplish the office's mission cost-effectively. In addition, OOI has not demonstrated the need to retain the current number of criminal investigators.

According to OPM's August 2009 *Introduction to the Position Classification Standards 2009*, OPM and Federal agencies are responsible for carrying out the classification system in accordance with the principles set forth in law. Federal managers are responsible for organizing work to accomplish the agency's mission most efficiently and economically. The Federal Government's policy is to use available resources optimally in assigning work.

Although OPM has overall responsibility for establishing the basic policies and guidance governing position classification and management for most Federal agencies, TSA is exempt from OPM classifications.[10] TSA has established its own position classifications and classification management procedures. However, with respect to law enforcement, TSA's policy is to adhere to OPM requirements so that TSA criminal investigators will be entitled to enhanced retirement benefits. Without OPM's approval, TSA criminal investigators would not qualify for enhanced retirement benefits covered in 5 USC Chapters 83–85 because TSA is not exempt from these provisions.[11] These benefits are only provided to those law enforcement personnel who are covered under the statutory and regulatory definitions of "law enforcement officer."

TSA is required to submit to OPM a list of law enforcement positions, separating the primary and secondary positions.[12] To ensure compliance with OPM regulations for law enforcement retirement benefits, TSA must also establish and maintain a file for each law enforcement officer with the position classification, the officer's actual duties, and all background material used to make the determination; OPM has the authority to audit these files.[13] Additionally, OPM can respond to requests for interpretations of classification issues and advisory opinions. Although OPM does not have the authority to require TSA to reclassify positions, OPM may determine that positions have been misclassified and therefore do not qualify for law enforcement retirement benefits.

In our opinion, as a subject matter expert, OPM can help TSA ensure that OOI law enforcement positions are properly classified according to statutes and regulations. This could help establish an efficient and cost-conscious organizational structure for OOI. Noting that OOI took no action to reclassify position misclassifications previously identified by OHC and its contractor, we believe that OPM would be the best organization to conduct this work independently and objectively. Without an objective and comprehensive workforce analysis of law enforcement position designations, OOI cannot ensure that it is using its staff and funding as efficiently as possible.

---

[9] Criminal investigators who receive LEAP pursuant to 5 USC § 5545(a) are exempt from the overtime provisions in the *Fair Labor Standards Act of 1938*, as amended, but may still receive overtime pay per Title 5 of the USC.

[10] 49 USC § 40122(g).

[11] 49 USC § 40122(g)(2)(G).

[12] 5 CFR § 842.808(a).

[13] 5 CFR § 842.808(c).

PLANNING, PERFORMANCE, AND QUALITY CONTROL

OOI did not effectively plan its work, did not adequately measure its performance, and did not have quality control procedures to ensure that all divisions complied with standards that the office had committed to using in its work. OOI also could not require other TSA offices to respond to its recommendations. In addition, TSA did not hold OOI accountable for developing and implementing effective quality controls over its resources, staffing, and operations. As a result of the issues that we identified with OOI's quality controls over its work products, TSA management may not be able to rely on this work, and the office may not have accomplished its mission to identify and address transportation security vulnerabilities.

OOI did not create an annual work plan to identify projects for each division to complete and the resources needed for each project. OOI divisions were not required to submit annual work plans for approval to ensure that OOI's planned work was consistent with TSA's priorities. Without an approved plan, OOI may not have been held accountable for accomplishing planned projects and could not effectively measure its annual performance.

OOI did not establish adequate performance measures or set standards to demonstrate its improvement over time. The office also did not create outcome-based performance measures, which would compare the results of its activities with the intended purpose, to assess its operations. Although OOI collected data to measure each division's output, such as the number of recommendations made, the number of offices inspected, and new investigations opened, these measures did not tie output to goals. During our audit, OOI indicated that it would begin to include more outcome-based metrics in its performance measures.

Without an annual work plan and without adequate outcome-based performance measures, OOI could not prepare an annual budget plan based on proposed work. Although OOI submitted a spending plan to TSA based on historical data, including its salary obligations, travel, contracts, and training, it did not track actual spending against the plan. Without a work plan as a basis for an annual budget plan, OOI was unable to demonstrate that it was effectively managing and distributing its resources.

OOI did not have accurate information on project costs. Not all OOI personnel were required to record hours spent on projects or report other resource-related information in the existing data management system, and use of the system varied by division. Recording project hours provides the basis for estimating and tracking project costs. Without consistent use of the data management system, OOI could not accurately measure project costs and could not ensure efficient use of resources.

OOI did not establish quality control procedures to ensure that all its divisions complied with applicable professional standards, such as *Government Auditing Standards* and the *Council of the Inspectors General on Integrity and Efficiency Quality Standards for Inspection and Evaluation*. Although OOI is not required to follow these standards, the office committed to using them in conducting its work. For instance, although during our audit it took steps to comply, the Internal Review Division had not been externally peer-reviewed as required by *Government Auditing Standards*.

To determine air carriers' compliance with 9/11 security fee requirements, OOI conducts audits in accordance with *Government Auditing Standards*. For audits that meet all applicable requirements in *Government Auditing Standards*, OOI should include a compliance statement in the report. For audits that do not meet all applicable requirements, OOI should include a modified compliance statement in the report identifying the requirement or requirements that were not met. Consequently, until a peer review is completed, all OOI reports claiming to meet *Government Auditing Standards* should have modified statements.

OOI also did not have policies and procedures to ensure that its staff members met these standards' training requirements to maintain technical proficiency. Following these standards would help OOI operate more efficiently and effectively and would enhance its credibility.

OOI supervisors in the office's three operational divisions did not adequately review the supporting work papers for reports of inspections, covert testing, and internal reviews. Of the 29 reports issued between fiscal year 2010 and the first quarter of fiscal year 2012 that we reviewed, only 6 had evidence of supervisory review. Supervisory review ensures that the work performed has met its objectives and that the findings, conclusions, and recommendations are adequately supported. Without consistent supervisory review, OOI could not ensure the quality of its reports or that it had adequately identified and addressed security vulnerabilities.

OOI did not have effective quality controls on data entry and review in its management information system; therefore, it could not be certain of the accuracy and reliability of its trend analyses and updates on the status of its operations. For example, misspelling words in the system could result in employees not identifying all of the investigations in a query when totaling the number of investigations. In October 2011, after receiving conflicting information on the number of investigations OOI had completed, the TSA deputy administrator at the time identified data accuracy as an issue.

OOI's recommendations resulting from its inspections, covert testing, and internal reviews were not always implemented. According to an OOI official, TSA offices were not required to respond to or implement OOI's recommendations because OOI did not have the authority to require compliance with its recommendations. OOI also did not have a formalized process to monitor responses and implementation of recommendations or a resolution process to resolve instances of nonconcurrence. As a result, TSA may have missed opportunities to address transportation security vulnerabilities.

RECOMMENDATIONS

We made 11 recommendations to TSA that, when implemented, should lead to more efficient and effective operations, improve transparency and accountability, and enhance efforts to protect the Nation's transportation systems. TSA concurred with all of our recommendations. In late December 2013, we received updates from TSA on some of the recommendations, which we are currently reviewing. Below are the recommendations and their current status.

Our first four recommendations related to OOI's criminal investigators.

We recommended that the assistant administrator for OOI:

> 1. Ensure that OOI criminal investigators in primary positions meet the Federal 50 percent minimum workload requirement and meet all LEAP requirements as a condition of receiving this premium pay.
>
> Recommendation 1 is unresolved and will remain open until OOI provides documentation showing how it will ensure that its criminal investigators are meeting the legal requirement to spend at least 50 percent of their time conducting criminal investigations, which is required to qualify them as law enforcement officers and make them eligible for LEAP. In its response to our report, TSA did not specifically state how it will ensure criminal investigators meet this requirement.
>
> 2. Finalize and implement OOI's management directive on LEAP policies and procedures to require all employees receiving LEAP to document their work hours in the OOI database.
>
> Recommendation 2 is resolved and closed. TSA has directed that all employees who receive LEAP must document their work hours.

We also recommended that the TSA Deputy Administrator:

> 3. Conduct an objective workforce analysis of OOI, including a needs assessment, and perform a position classification review, ensuring that those conducting the review, such OHC or OPM, are independent of the process.
>
> Recommendation 3 is unresolved and open. In its response, TSA agreed to have a workforce analysis conducted of OOI, but that analysis will be limited to the Audits and Inspection Division and the Security Operations Division. TSA made no mention of an analysis of the criminal investigators in the Internal Affairs Division, which at the time of our audit, comprised approximately 82 percent of the total number of OOI criminal investigators.
>
> 4. Upon completion of the workforce analysis and position classification review, reclassify criminal investigator primary positions that do not or are not expected to meet the Federal workload requirement. In addition, ensure that secondary law enforcement positions are properly classified in accordance with Federal regulations. Proper classification of supervisors depends on correctly classifying the individuals they supervise.
>
> Recommendation 4 is unresolved and open. Although TSA agreed to a workforce analysis, it will be limited to the Audits and Inspection Division and the Security Operations Division.

To improve the quality of OOI's inspections, covert testing, and internal reviews, we recommended that the assistant administrator for OOI:

> 5. Require OOI to develop a detailed annual work plan to be approved by the assistant administrator, which contains project-specific information, including purpose, duration, realistic cost estimates, and required staffing.

Recommendation 5 is resolved and open. In its response TSA stated that OOI has developed a work plan for the Audits and Inspection Division and Special Operations Division. These plans will be combined into one plan for approval by OOI's assistant administrator. TSA provided its response and proposed implementation plan for corrective action. We are currently evaluating TSA's response.

6. Ensure that OOI develops outcome-based performance measures for its programs, projects, and operations to evaluate efficiency and effectiveness.

Recommendation 6 is unresolved and open. TSA responded that OOI has developed overall performance metrics for the office. In reviewing TSA's corrective action plan, we believe the proposed action does not fully address the intent of the recommendation because it focuses on goals rather than outcome-based performance measures. The recommendation will remain open until TSA provides documentation to support that OOI has developed and implemented outcome-based performance measures that evaluate the efficiency and effectiveness of the office.

7. Periodically assess the results of OOI's performance measures to assess progress toward meeting the intended goals and revise programs as necessary.

Recommendation 7 is resolved and open. TSA responded that OOI tracks conformance to performance measures quarterly and annually and will continue to track the outcomes. This recommendation will remain open until OOI provides documentation that it periodically assesses outcome-based performance measures, not only goals, for its programs, projects, and operations to evaluate their efficiency and effectiveness.

8. Ensure that OOI requires staff members to document hours spent on projects in its management information system, and ensure that criminal investigators document hours to support LEAP.

Recommendation 8 is resolved and open. TSA provided its response and proposed implementation plan for corrective action. We are currently evaluating TSA's response.

9. Establish a quality assurance program to ensure that OOI complies with applicable professional standards such as *Government Auditing Standards* and the *Council of the Inspectors General on Integrity and Efficiency Quality Standards for Inspection and Evaluation.* This program should include:

• Tests of the quality and reliability of data in the office's management information system.

• Evidence that staff meet continuing professional education requirements.

• Documentation of staff's independence for each project.

• Quality control reviews to ensure that the work products meet professional standards.

For recommendation 9, TSA provided its response and proposed implementation plan for corrective action. We are currently evaluating TSA's response.

10. Ensure that OOI expeditiously completes its action to have an external peer review of its efforts to audit air carriers and continues to have an external peer review of this work at least once every 3 years. Prior reports that did not comply with *Government Auditing Standards* need to be modified and reissued with language that OOI was not fully compliant with *Government Auditing Standards* when the audits were conducted.

Recommendation 10 is resolved and open. TSA provided its response and proposed implementation plan for corrective action. We are currently evaluating TSA's response.

11. Develop and implement a policy for recommendation follow-up and resolution to ensure that other TSA offices respond to all of OOI's recommendations, and establish a resolution process when offices do not concur with recommendations.

Recommendation 11 is resolved and open. TSA has provided its response and proposed implementation plan for corrective action. We are currently evaluating TSA's response.

Mr. Chairman, this concludes my prepared statement. I welcome any questions you or other Members of the subcommittee may have.

Mr. HUDSON. Thank you, Ms. Richards.

We appreciate all of you being here today.

At this point I will recognize the Ranking Minority Member of the subcommittee, the gentleman from Louisiana, Mr. Richmond, for his opening statement.

Mr. RICHMOND. Thank you, Chairman Hudson.

Let me just thank you for convening this hearing, and the witnesses for appearing today and for your testimony.

As you all know, the work that this subcommittee does is extremely important. We are tasked with making sure that the Transportation Security Administration fulfills its mission of protecting the Nation's transportation systems to ensure freedom of movement for our people and our commerce.

More importantly, we are tasked with ensuring the safety of American citizens as they travel across this Nation. To accomplish this mission we must ensure that every office within the Transportation Security Administration is operating both effectively and efficiently.

The report released in September 2013 by the Department of Homeland Security's Office of Inspector General regarding the Office of Inspection is both alarming and scathing. The report details that the Office of Inspection is not operating at maximum efficiency or in a cost-effective manner because of a top-heavy structure.

Specifically, the Office of Inspection employs personnel classified as criminal investigators despite their duties not fitting the classification of criminal investigations according to Federal regulations. This classification allows these criminal investigators to receive enhanced benefits and LEAP pay. According to the OIG report and, as I understand it, two prior reports, substantial savings could be achieved by reclassifying these criminal investigators in a manner consistent with the needs of the Office of Inspection and the type of work they perform.

Undoubtedly, there are many examples of instances in which the Office of Inspection has helped thwart the efforts of nefarious actors who mean to do our Nation harm. That, however, does not diminish the need for us to use our resources effectively so that we can operate at maximum efficiency.

It is my hope that through the questions and testimony we gather today we can get further insight about where these inefficiencies are occurring, how we can reallocate our resources in an effective manner, and also what can be done structurally within the TSA so that when these structural problems are first brought to light they can be quickly addressed.

I look forward to the continued dialogue and hope that the work that we do here today aids in making the Transportation Security Administration stronger, more efficient, and more effective.

Before yielding back I would like to note that this is the first hearing of the subcommittee in the second session of this Congress. It is my expectation that this subcommittee will be as bipartisan and productive this year as it was last year, when our subcommittee produced four out of the five bills that the committee saw pass the House.

I look forward to continuing to work with the Chairman to see that the bills we sent to the Senate in December, including Ranking Member Thompson's bill to codify the aviation security advisory committee, becomes law this year.

With that, Mr. Chairman, I will yield back.

Mr. HUDSON. Thank the gentleman, and I thank you for the comments. I share the sentiment that we want to continue to work in a bipartisan way to find solutions for the American people here.

At this point I will recognize myself for questions.

The I.G. report states that TSA could save $17.5 million over the next 5 years if it reclassified the criminal investigators to non-law enforcement positions. According to the I.G., the amount of criminal cases conducted every year does not support all the TSA's criminal investigators so reclassifying these positions is necessary and appropriate.

Mr. Allison, do you agree with the I.G.'s assessment that employees in non-law enforcement positions like transportation security specialist can perform the work of most of your 100 criminal investigators? Why or why not?

Mr. ALLISON. Thank you, Mr. Chairman.

Actually, I do disagree with a certain point of that. I mean, when you look at this type of work, what is pretty much consistent in this field is tracking your hours against the cases, so admittedly the organization did not track its hours. So if the investigators were working criminal cases or administrative cases and they did not track their hours one wouldn't be able to tell what their workload was.

So, for example, the 1,125 cases that the Office of Investigations for the I.G. reviewed in 2011, they identified some 40 percent that were collateral, meaning cases that other agencies investigated. But I would submit to you, Mr. Chairman, that those cases represent the most minimal amount of time because anytime someone is arrested, indicted, or under investigation by another law enforcement agency, given our mission, those people are a threat or a risk to our security mission.

So what is pretty consistent in this career field is you would open a case and that is how we monitor those individual cases. So although they identified 423 cases, or some 40 percent of the 1,125, without the time you wouldn't know if that constituted a majority of the workload.

I will contend, having experience in this business, that the majority of the workload was divided between the criminal cases and the administrative cases and less to the 423. But again, I just want to acknowledge that, you know, our organization erred in not tracking those hours and you would not be able to discern what the workload truly was, so at first glance you would assume, given those 423 cases, a lot of work went there, but not necessarily the case.

So I do believe we can, you know, through this analysis, take a look at our work through predictive analysis, through some of the work we have already done, and make a determination if we need to, you know, reduce the numbers of some of our investigative staff.

Mr. HUDSON. But to do these types of review where another agency is doing the investigation and your folks are monitoring, do you need the law enforcement classification to do that—1811 versus some other classification?

Mr. ALLISON. I am sorry, Mr. Chairman. Yes, I mean, we can reduce some of our staff and augment our staff with non-criminal investigators, there is no question, because all that information is coming back and it is being recorded and the cases are being updated, so yes.

Mr. HUDSON. So of the 100, how many do you think we could reduce out of that category?

Mr. ALLISON. Well, Mr. Chairman, as I stated in my opening statement, since I have been there I have reduced by 6 percent. I believe we can reduce further. I don't have an accurate account for you. I mean, I am confident that we can attrit some of our positions.

Mr. HUDSON. Okay.

Ms. Richards, would you like to comment on this response, or——

Ms. RICHARDS. I would like to comment.

Yes, one of the main concerns is, as Mr. Allison says, the Office of Inspections was not having its employees record what they were actually doing so it was impossible to discern with certitude how many hours were spent on a criminal investigation versus an administrative investigation or on a collateral investigation or on an inspection or an internal review or covert testing. One of our recommendations to which they have agreed and taken action is to start recording exactly what the employees are doing, which will help them tremendously evaluate their workforce and complete the workforce analysis that we have asked them to do.

It is also our contention that they could reduce the number of criminal investigators they have and that, for example, the collateral investigations could be conducted by non-criminal investigators.

Mr. HUDSON. Thank you.

In order to enforce the time limits I am going to enforce them on myself and go ahead and conclude my questions and call on the Ranking Minority Member of the subcommittee, the gentleman from Louisiana, Mr. Richmond for any questions he may have.

Mr. RICHMOND. Well, let me start with Ms. Richards where you just left off and the fact that they didn't accurately track their hours. I guess my question is: If they are not tracking their hours and they don't adequately say what their hours are going to and what case they are assigned to and all of that, how do you feel confident in your numbers? Because I guess we would all rely on the same reporting in order to draw conclusions, so I guess I am wondering, how did you draw your conclusions since they are not doing that?

Ms. RICHARDS. Our Office of Investigations had done an inspection of their criminal investigators and analyzed the workload that was completed. We also know what types of cases we refer to TSA.

As you are aware, the Office of Inspector General has primacy on cases—criminal cases involving Department of Homeland Security employees, so TSA shows us the cases and when they are truly criminal or serious nature in general, our office takes those cases on and we refer back to TSA cases that are administrative in nature or what they call de minimis, which would mean that the

cases were for an issue that was minor in nature and would be un-
likely to be accepted for prosecution as a criminal case.

Mr. RICHMOND. Ms. Shelton Waters, let me shift over to you, and
I know you haven't been there a very, very long time, but I would
assume that you are there because you are very good. Part of what
I guess my question to you is just an assessment whether your office has the internal capacity to do inspections and reviews on your
own or are you going to need to continue to contract out to have
others do inspections?

Ms. SHELTON WATERS. Thank you for the question, sir. So I think
absolutely internally we have the ability, we have the subject-matter expertise to lend to the overall discussion.

Our model right now, though, really is to have contractor support
for what we do in OHC and it is a model that we have had for the
last 9 years or so. So my staff is about 200 right now and that includes all of my FTE. But again, we use contractor support to augment or to supplement what we do there.

So whatever work we end up doing with OOI—and we absolutely
plan to be very robust in how we go about figuring out the right
mix—the right levels of 1811s versus the other workforce that OOI
needs to accomplish their mission—we will continue to rely on contractor support for that.

Mr. RICHMOND. Do you think contractor support is the most efficient way to do it? I guess the reason why I am asking—and this
is not my area of subject-matter expertise—that when you contract
it out you get the result or the report that you are looking for but
there is—that ends the on-going and long-term dialogue and coordi-
nation between agencies; and if you were able to do it in-house
then you would have the same people there over the long term who
could hopefully interact and monitor progress without having to go
back to contractors.

Ms. SHELTON WATERS. So I don't disagree with your assessment.
One of the things that I looked at in the first 30 days that I was
in the Office of Human Capital was how we want to build our
model for the future.

The contract support that we currently have—the overarching
contract support—expires at the beginning of 2017. My goal is to
position us for what I consider to be a less risk—or a more risk-
based approach, meaning that I will have a better understanding
of the mix of Federal-to-contractor support than what I have today,
and that will be our model moving forward.

Mr. RICHMOND. Mr. Allison, it is my understanding and just my
opinion that everybody at the table, everybody up here, we are all
on the same team, although sometimes I differ from my colleagues
on the other side of the aisle, but we are all on the same team and
we want to be as efficient and productive as possible.

It appears to me, just looking at the reports, unless you can just
tell me, "Something is flat-out wrong. We don't have efficiencies
there. Other people can't do these criminal investigations, and we
are not paying too much in LEAP pay and others," why can't we
all get together and figure out what is the appropriate number,
how much we can save so that we can take those savings and put
it right back into homeland security or making the traveling public
easier, reducing—I mean, I just don't understand how, if we are all

on the same team, why we don't get together and fix it? Can you explain that to me?

Mr. ALLISON. Sure, Mr. Richmond.

I don't disagree. I mean, in these times we need to look within our organizations and be more efficient, when we can, where we can. The reason we reduced by 6 percent was just through that process. You know, I didn't have a report at the time when I walked in the door. Any time I have a vacancy the question I ask is: "Do we still need this position? Do we still need this position at that grade?"

So you are right. We have an obligation to be as efficient as we can.

With respect to this problem, sir, there were various reports but again, I would contend what is missing from this equation, as you alluded to, without time attached to these numbers they don't tell the whole story. So again, you know, a case is just a file and it may not represent any time at all other than just an update.

So to the Chairman's point, do you need an investigator—a criminal investigator for that percentage of workload that you know you are always going to have? The question comes: How do we balance our cadre of folks? Do we attrit down to a certain number and augment with non-criminal or do we just attrit down to a number and have those positions and work be done and contained as long as people are abiding by the law?

So I don't disagree with you. I think this process that we are about to embark upon, you know, analyzing this data, recognizing the I.G.'s responsibility—you know, the cases that they take and the cases that they don't take. As I alluded in my opening statement, they took 3 percent of the cases—of the 423 that we referred last year.

I would disagree with my colleague; it has nothing to do with whether it prosecutes or not, they don't have the capacity to do this work. Their report to Congress for 2012 basically alludes to the fact that they refer a lot of cases back to the components for investigation.

So we certainly need to have a cadre. One hundred is probably not the right number; it is certainly not zero. We are going to work and, you know, I assure you, we are going to fix this problem.

Mr. HUDSON. Thank you.

The Chairman will now recognize other Members of the committee for questions they may wish to ask the witness. In accordance with our committee rules and practices, I plan to recognize Members who were present at the start of the hearing by seniority on the subcommittee. Those coming in later will be recognized in the order of arrival.

At this time I will recognize the gentleman from Alabama, Mr. Rogers.

Mr. ROGERS. Thank you, Mr. Chairman.

You know, the Senate is having a hearing similar to this today and it has been pointed out over there that tracking overtime is a problem Department-wide. Is that something you would agree with or do you think it is just happening in your Department—TSA?

Mr. ALLISON. Thank you, Mr. Rogers.

Again, no question OOI did not track their hours against cases—I mean, allocating hours towards the cases, that did not happen. They did track their law enforcement availability pay hours, meaning the 2 hours they must be available every day, on hard copy. That wasn't available in an automated fashion. But they did not track the hours, so a little bit of a different problem.

Mr. ROGERS. Okay. The I.G. recommended in its report that TSA conduct a workforce analysis to determine the appropriate OOI staffing levels. TSA stated that it would conduct this analysis for the audits and inspections division and the security operations divisions of OOI; however, there is no indication that TSA will analyze the internal affairs division, which contains over 80 percent of OOI's criminal investigations.

Mr. Allison and Ms. Waters, why is TSA not including the internal affairs division in its upcoming workforce analysis?

Ms. Waters first.

Ms. SHELTON WATERS. So I don't think that we are opposed to including that part of OOI in that analysis. I believe—and I apologize for not having the full information on that—I believe that there was an understanding at the time that that was done that the numbers that were being questioned were in those two divisions.

But as Mr. Allison indicated, whether it is through this particular contract support or through the tools that we have in OHC, we do plan to do a full analysis of the Office of Inspections to understand what the right mix of workforce levels should be.

Mr. ROGERS. Mr. Allison, do you have anything to add?

Mr. ALLISON. No, sir. I completely agree. I mean, we are going to embark upon this endeavor to do this analysis. You know, we need to include the full cadre of criminal investigators so I have no objection to that and I think it is a good idea.

Mr. ROGERS. Ms. Richards, do you have a comment? Do you think that it is important for the internal affairs division to be looked at?

Ms. RICHARDS. Absolutely. I think it is critically important as part of the workforce analysis that the entire office be looked at.

Mr. ROGERS. Okay. Ms. Richards, in your view, what entity is in the best position to conduct an objective, comprehensive analysis of OOI's workforce and give clear direction on how to fix the problem?

Ms. RICHARDS. As we stated in our report, we believe that OPM would be the best entity within the Government to do this workforce analysis and the reason that we believe that is because previous studies by OHC and a contractor working for OHC reached conclusions that were similar to those that we reached with our audit work but those reports, although they made recommendations, were disagreed with, and the recommendations were not implemented.

Mr. ROGERS. Okay. In your opinion, Ms. Richards, should TSA have the unique authority to set its own employee classifications or should it be brought under OPM's employee classification system?

Ms. RICHARDS. That is a really broad question. Based on our limited audit work I wouldn't be prepared to answer it at this time. I do have concerns with this particular office that we audited that they need to do a thorough workforce analysis and bring it in line with what is appropriate for the workload that they have.

Mr. ROGERS. I would like you to revisit the question I asked Mr. Allison at the beginning of my time, and that is: Do you think that the problem with tracking overtime is unique to TSA or do you think it is across the whole Department of Homeland Security?

Ms. RICHARDS. In regards to administratively uncontrollable overtime, which is the subject of the other hearing, a number of those cases have been referred to the Office of Inspector General and we are just initiating our audit review of those cases. Based on what the special council has found, it does seem that there is a problem with AUO in the Department of Homeland Security.

It is slightly different than what is the problem in—that we are talking about in the Office of Inspection, but there are distinct similarities in that there seems to be a culture of entitlement that regardless of whether the specific work supports it or not or whether the documentation was there to support it or not, the money will be paid.

Mr. ROGERS. Great. Thank you.

I yield back, Mr. Chairman.

Mr. HUDSON. Thank the gentleman.

At this point the Chairman will recognize the gentleman from South Carolina, Mr. Sanford.

Mr. SANFORD. Yes. I just want to follow up again with Ms. Richards.

So if you look at the whole question of log books and hours, there has been a question raised here, if you look at the mismatch between criminal activity, number of criminal-related employees, and ultimately payroll budget, it seems like there is a mismatch there. In your findings, were there other mismatches that maybe didn't, you know, ultimately get surfaced in this audit but that were areas of concern that are worthy of conversation?

Ms. RICHARDS. I wouldn't say mismatch between employee skill sets and the duties that they were assigned. We had other concerns with the work that was being produced by the Office of Inspection.

For example, they were doing audits and saying the audits were conducted under Government auditing standards but they weren't meeting all of those standards. Some of the work didn't have indications of any supervisory review; the employees weren't necessarily receiving the training they needed to conduct these audits; they weren't always following the rules for documenting their independence.

So we had a number of issues with the other work that was being done but not necessarily with a mismatch between the skill sets of the employees and the work that was assigned them.

Mr. SANFORD. Why do you think—I would call it a mismatch; you wouldn't call it a mismatch—there was this overlay between demand, if you will, from a criminal investigative needs standpoint, and number of employees and compensation accrued? In your estimation, why did that exist?

Ms. RICHARDS. Looking back at how the office was stood up, I believe the anticipation was that they would need that many criminal investigators and that was never thoroughly examined in the history of the office. So, having stood the office up that way, they continued to grow it that way; that is the kind of individual that they hired and they attracted and that they used for the work that they considered important because these are good, solid employees and they felt that they were getting a good, solid product.

Without doing a workforce analysis and really seeing whether they were meeting the requirements for the law enforcement pay and entitlements, they were paying people probably more than they should have been because they weren't doing that work.

It is easy to see how the office was stood up in a hurry when TSA was stood up, but over the years that the office has existed they had, in my opinion, more than adequate time to do a workforce analysis and determine what their workload really was, and I believe they should have done so but they did not.

Mr. SANFORD. This, in your opinion, was not just a sloppy way of basically paying people more?

Ms. RICHARDS. I didn't find any evidence of that. I didn't find any evidence of intentional wrongdoing. I found evidence that they believed this was appropriate, and lacking the data to say differently and perhaps not the attention to detail that an auditor would give to determining all of the detailed information that would support their decision making.

Mr. SANFORD. How about throughput—the number of prosecutions that actually occurred? Did you look at that into the equation in your study, as well?

Ms. RICHARDS. We did not. Our Office of Investigations had recently looked at the workload of the criminal investigators and so we did not evaluate the quality of the workload or the results of those.

Mr. SANFORD. I am not saying quality, but just quantity, if you will. I mean——

Ms. RICHARDS. I don't have the statistics with me. I could get them for you.

Mr. SANFORD. No, no, no.

Mr. Allison, would you have counterpoint to what she said or——

Mr. ALLISON. Yes. Thank you, Mr. Congressman.

I do agree that some quantitative analysis should have occurred at some point to give us some baseline as to how many of these individuals that we should have. I would agree with her.

I came up in the Federal Marshal Service from TSA since 2002. I don't know what led to the number of, you know, whatever it was—when I walked into the job it was 106. The I.G. report quoted 124 but we are at 100 now, so this is where we are now.

So I do agree some sort of analysis should have been done, but I think, like I said before, sir, not documenting our hours, not accounting for our work is not the same as not doing the work. So last year we—I think we closed 887 cases; about 70 percent of those cases really were violations of criminal laws of the United States. Of the ones we——

Mr. SANFORD. How many prosecutions came as a result?

Mr. ALLISON. Sir, I have to get back to you on that information, I will provide it for you. I want to say around 18 or so—a very low number. But, sir, as you know, I mean, those are subject to DOJ guidelines and prosecutorial thresholds and all that stuff.

Mr. SANFORD. I see I burned through my time.

Thank you, Mr. Chairman.

Mr. HUDSON. Thank the gentleman.

I will now recognize the gentlelady from Indiana, Mrs. Brooks.

Mrs. BROOKS. Thank you, Mr. Chairman. Thanks for holding this hearing.

When you talk about TSA and when it was stood up and how it has changed over the years, I happen to have been a United States attorney, Southern District of Indiana, when TSA was stood up, so I have kind of watched—and served from 2001 until 2007, so watched TSA grow, was a part of conversations in Indiana in supporting TSA and, you know, want to thank you all for your service and what, you know, how important it is. I defend TSA with constituents day in and day out about the importance of keeping this country safe.

I also, though, know that the number of prosecution cases the U.S. Attorney's Office, you know, takes are limited because of their limited resources, but I do think there was a response—TSA did respond—I am just following up on Congressman Sanford's point. OOI opened 582 criminal cases in 2012, 611 in 2013. Are you familiar with these numbers that—and of those cases, U.S. attorneys accepted 12 for prosecution in 2012 and then 18 in 2013.

Can you help us understand what seems to be the problems— and I have been on the other side of the U.S. attorney making those decisions and with an office making the decisions about what to prosecute and what not to prosecute, but I am kind of—they do seem to be fairly low numbers. For the numbers that are opened, if you are opening hundreds and it is not minimizing the work that is going into it, but what has happened with the Justice Department and the guidelines—what are the guidelines they are using to have to decide—or what have they told you the guidelines are to decide whether or not to prosecute or not?

Mr. ALLISON. Yes, ma'am. I do not know unequivocally. When we got that request we did get some data from our supervisors in the field and I directed a 100 percent accounting of the casework to— so we can look at every individual case through 2011 and 2012 and get an accurate accounting so I can report back to the committee.

But to your prominent question, a lot of our criminal cases are thefts. From my experience in the year-and-a-half I have been in this office I think, you know, they would defer for administrative resolution.

We do get some prosecutions on OWCP cases. Those are typically the larger amounts of cases. Those cases aren't accepted by the DHS OIG; those are always returned back to TSA.

Mrs. BROOKS. I am sorry, what kind of cases are those?

Mr. ALLISON. Office of Worker's Compensation fraud. I am sorry, ma'am.

Mrs. BROOKS. Okay.

Mr. ALLISON. Most of those cases—all of those cases go back to TSA, so we had a few prosecutions in that area. One of the prosecutions we had this year in the District of Maryland was time theft—fairly large amount related to time theft.

So typically, the larger dollar amounts seem to get the interest of prosecutions where the lower dollar amounts do not.

Mrs. BROOKS. So of those prosecutions, were those typically done by your agency alone or were those with other investigative agencies involved?

Mr. ALLISON. Ma'am, they would have been our agency.

Mrs. BROOKS. So have the prosecutors said there is a monetary threshold because of their sentencing guidelines that is then determining whether or not they are taking the cases or not taking the cases?

Mr. ALLISON. Ma'am, I would contend that it varies upon the district. You know, some districts like New York have a very high threshold for prosecution that are extremely busy; some—in Nevada, you know, they prosecuted a gentleman, I think, for stealing a pair of boots. So it varies.

Mrs. BROOKS. So if there are those disparities across the districts—and I appreciate that that does happen—when they get sent back, they are not prosecuted in the district courts, have you produced any reports—and I am just sorry that I don't know—as to what happens to all of those theft cases involving TSA employees that aren't prosecuted? How are they being handled within the agency?

Mr. ALLISON. Well, that is a great question. I will assure you that those cases go over to Office of OPR and those people generally on theft cases are dismissed.

Mrs. BROOKS. So general theft cases are dismissed by OPR?

Mr. ALLISON. Well, no. I mean, the—I am sorry, the employees are dismissed——

Mrs. BROOKS. The employees, okay. Thank you. I wanted to clarify.

Mr. ALLISON. So once our investigations are concluded, if they are declined for prosecution those go to my colleague at OPR and they actually render administrative discipline on those cases.

Mrs. BROOKS. Is that an annual report that we would have ability to review and to take a look at to see what is happening with all of those other cases that are not being referred for criminal prosecution? Is that in a report form?

Mr. ALLISON. I will be happy to give you a report——

Mrs. BROOKS. Okay.

Mr. ALLISON [continuing]. And show you what we have done with the cases over the years, and to the ones to your question that aren't prosecuted.

Mrs. BROOKS. Just very briefly, one case that was prosecuted which I think is an incredibly important case that I am curious about the skill sets of the investigator, the case from 2009 involving the logic bomb that was actually inserted into the TSA system—the computer program file of the TSA operation system. Do you feel that we have the investigators properly trained to detect the cyber crime within TSA or cyber terrorism within TSA?

Mr. ALLISON. Well, two points, ma'am. Typically an allegation of that would get referred to the I.G., and I think that one did, and we had to actually exercise, as I understand—I wasn't there at the time—you know, some very quick response to mitigate this issue. So with the investigator we had some I.T. professionals and we had a computer forensics agent and I think those folks went to Colorado Springs and worked that case and were able to resolve that issue successfully.

Mrs. BROOKS. Well, I would be interested in knowing how many of all of these investigators that we have actually have the expertise. That is a very important area that I think the whole country is very concerned about and I would be very curious—investigating thefts of baggage and other things, dramatically different skill set than investigation of the computer—the TSA computers and any, you know, cyber issues there.

So I would love to know and would ask that you provide for us what kind of training your investigators are also getting with respect to cyber crime.

I have exceeded my time and yield back. Thank you.

Mr. HUDSON. Thank the gentlelady.

I want to thank the witnesses for your testimony, for your service to our country.

I am very pleased we were able to get through the hearing before they called votes. Thank the Members for their questions and participation today.

The Members of the subcommittee may have some additional questions for the witnesses and we ask that you respond to these in writing.

Without objection, the subcommittee stands adjourned.

[Whereupon, at 2:20 p.m., the subcommittee was adjourned.]

○

www.ingramcontent.com/pod-product-compliance
Lightning Source LLC
Chambersburg PA
CBHW080737290526
45790CB00008B/3227